CAMELIA ELIAS

# THE HEART SUTRA

&

 TAROT

EYECORNER PRESS

*The Heart Sutra and Tarot* © Camelia Elias 2020.
Published by EyeCorner Press. Designed and
typeset by Camelia Elias. Images: Jean Noblet
Marseille Tarot, 1650, as reconstructed by Jean-
Claude Flornoy. By kind permission from Susanne
Flornoy; A Sanskrit fragment of the Heart Sutra,
courtesy of Bibliothèque nationale de France.

ISBN: 978-87-92633-70-5
December 2020, Agger, Denmark

EYECORNERPRESS.COM

*For my sister, Manna*

# Contents

## The Gift of Attendance

E VERY NOW AND THEN I decide to
be-gift myself the gift of my own words that
I then be-gift to others. The text in front of
you is the result of a lecture on *The Heart Sutra
and the Tarot* presented for an audience of 77
people, followed also by a Q&A session.

After having archived the material in 2016,
I found myself returning to it. A word kept
resonating in my head: coping. 2020 was a bitter
cup for many; a year of coping. As the pandemic
set in, some got poor, some got rich, some died,

and others were left to coping. 'How do we get beyond this?' many wanted to know, and the more this question presented itself, the more I thought about *The Heart Sutra*. As this is a text that prompts us with thinking about the beyond, I started asking the big questions:

What is beyond good and evil?
What is beyond moral and immoral?
What is beyond love and hate?
What is beyond you and me?

The reason why we want to go beyond is because it's possible, especially if we attend to the idea. How? My work with the cards can be said to be all about attendance. It also starts with a line of investigations:

How do I attend to my question?
How do I attend to how I formulate it?
How do I attend to paying attention?
How do I attend to who I am?

Let me combine the two here, my love of texts that attend to the beyond, and my love of cards that attend to our astonishments.

The beyond manifests as the heart of the
supernatural, which is the ordinary in the
extraordinary. Why else do you suppose you
can speak with the dead, divine for your future
with the cards, or give clear and precise answers
to yourself and others on current concerns or
old wounds? Because the more the heart opens
up, the more what it opens up to is receiving
the gift of grace. Which you don't control.
Sorry for the bad news.

The more you aspire to unification, the
alchemical integration of your parts and pieces
of yourself that you're not aware of, the more
you place yourself in attendance. It is the rule
of all spirituality that you don't receive the
gift of grace because you can make an effort to
hone your mediumistic, cartomantic, magic,
witchy, or Zen skills. No. Experiencing the
supernatural, the precise real in your heart, is
contingent on your ability to place yourself in

attendance. When the heart opens itself up to the beyond, you find that you rest in attendance to what you're doing every single moment. That in itself is the beyond, the meditation, the spontaneous observation of the obvious, or the so-called path of the spirit walkers.

Resting in attendance is also the only challenge, for resting in attendance doesn't require a schedule: 'I'll do it tonight, when the moon is waning and Jupiter makes a trine to Venus. I'll do it on All Hallows Eve, when the veil between the worlds is thin. I'll do it tomorrow, when my body is relaxed, and my new cool Halloween costume has arrived from China.'

You can do all these things as part of your devotion, but none of it is required for the actual experience of the supernatural, the real in the ordinary, such as listening to a bird singing just as you get in your car to rush to work or decoding messages in the smoke dedicated to Papa Legba or Lucifer on a Tuesday instead of a Monday.

What resting in attendance *does* require is your constant presence without grasping at belief or effort. Resting in attendance requires your paying attention. Plain and simple.

So far, so good. The more you pay attention, the more you see the obvious. When you see the obvious, you have clarity. When you have clarity, you're not ambivalent about which way to go. When you have direction, you have clear vision. Success.

'What success?' I'm not saying that this is the question that the short text of *The Heart Sutra* poses – which it does in a fragment I'll introduce you to shortly. What I'm saying is that *you* are asking, 'what success?' You are the one who has this question nagging, if you read the neat string of causal relations above: 'when you see the obvious, you have clarity, when you have clarity...' Success. *The Heart Sutra* says that there are no eyes, no ears, no mouth, there's no body. Who, or what then, attends to all this success? Who or what attends to the failure to cope with not sensing, or the realization that all things that are, *are not?* – that includes your being emotional about it.

In what follows I want to present you with a reading of a reading. A reading of *The Heart Sutra* through the lens of the 22 trumps of the Marseille Tarot. A reading about experiencing the supernatural at the heart of the natural, the extraordinary at the heart of the ordinary. But it is also about attending to things that we don't perceive, simply because we're not trained in perceiving anything at all. We are trained in imitating. Now imagine having the freedom to perceive beyond conditioning. Why aim for that? Because *that* is the highest magic: to perceive things beyond imitation.

My own experience of reading *The Heart Sutra* is quite terrible. It leaves me flat on the floor, lifeless. That is to say, after it first puts me in a vertigo state. My sensory nerves accelerate towards the kind of nothingness that leaves me utterly convinced that the body is quite the nothing itself compared to the idea. I can open my eyes, move my arms about, and talk. That's an experience. But of what? Of imitating. It's all performance and representation. Now what if I entertained the *idea* of purging imitation, or the idea that my uncontrollable ticks and movements are not even aesthetically interesting in any way whatsoever, in spite of what an army of theorists might try to convince me of otherwise? I hear all the claims: 'Your body is all there is,' 'your mind is all there is...' people divided into camps insist.

*The Heart Sutra* says, 'bugger off, if you insist on any of that nonsense.' I don't insist. I'll just give you the words, and then the image. I'll let the tarot attend to *The Heart Sutra,* and be as heartless about it as *The Heart Sutra* itself is about the heart. There's no heart...

But that's how we cope, knowing *that,* if coping is what we need. The minute we stop breathing life into useless beliefs, conceptual worlds, and cherished claims, we go beyond.

## When You're Done Fainting

**T**HE MILLION DOLLAR QUESTION: have you ever experienced the feeling that every time you got into something you really liked, you thought you liked, and you were convinced you were going to like until the end of your days, you discovered that this one thing or aspect of your life placed you in a position that stretched you, making you lose focus, even doubt what it was exactly that you liked to begin with? Welcome to the idea that there is nothing you can ever do other than just relax and accept what you are, beyond any conditioned notion of being, beyond any idiotic self-help notion that if only you were willing to risk yourself and sacrifice some shit, you would become a god, a goddess, or some other such useless conceptual entity based on words.

The promise of the illusion of *becoming* merely contributes to rendering you more miserable in a different way than what you have experienced so far.

### NO BEING, NO BECOMING

Sounds crazy, right? Culturally, this is crazy, for the whole point of culture is to instruct you in how you acquire an identity that you can cherish, nurture, and invest in.

After all, if the identity you get, or get accustomed to doesn't work, 'no worries,' culture will tell you, 'you can always change, shapeshift, transform, become, and in the process, invest some more in the new image of yourself.'

Hallelujah. But wait, isn't all this pretty crazy too? You bet. This is a lot crazier than the idea that you don't exist and don't become anything that you are not already. You are beyond being this or becoming that. Now you want to know: How can I be beyond being this or becoming that?

Am I not a man?

Am I not a woman?

If I am a man can I not become a woman?

If I am a woman can I not become a man?

If I am a shoemaker, like my great grandfather, can I not become a doctor if I study hard in these modern days of opportunities? My identity is not fixed... You hear the indignation.

The answer is you *can*, relatively speaking, because what you call a man, woman, a shoemaker, and doctor are all words, hence fictions, and we all know what we can do with words, what fictions we can create, and what conceptual images we can transact with, sell ourselves and others.

But, what if these images of self are devoid of all substance? What if 'myself' is devoid of all substance? What if what I call happiness and success is devoid of all substance? What if nothing has substance?

## WELCOME TO GOING BEYOND WHAT IF...

Welcome to getting curious about the beyond of all instruction on what you are, how you can change, and what you can become. Welcome to ditching the effort of rising to expectation, yours and others alike. Welcome to emptiness, your no-substance. Welcome to my no-substance. If you find yourself nodding, go further. Are you nodding in approval, or are you nodding because you understand? If the latter, then you're acting in accordance already. That is to say, you're your own person. For now...

Now pay attention. Salute yourself and take a deep breath. What we are dealing with, always, is this: nondualist perception. The perception that nothing has substance is not opposed to the dualist thinking whose value is created in the negative and in causality: 'I am a woman because I am *not* a man.'

If nondualist perception opposed dualism, it would submit to dualist thinking. This much is clear, as this statement has a premise in logical deduction. So what is nondualist perception, then? It's the perception that acknowledges the interconnectedness of all non-substance.

## CARTOMANTIC SUBSTANCE

Take your cards and ask them: 'what does it mean to say that nothing has substance?' Ask this question, however, with this awareness in mind: when you search for meaning you invariably submit to the world of dual relations that presupposes that there is something there you can find. If something has meaning, then this presupposes that there's something else out there that is devoid of meaning. That something has no meaning gives you purpose in your search for meaning. So you feel happy. For a moment. Until you realize this: 'meaning' and 'purpose' are just words made up of the purely symbolical glyphs of the alphabet.

'Meaning' and 'purpose' are not self-existing. They have no inherent meaning. They have no substance beyond the cultural conventions that have them appear to us thus: letters arranged in a specific order to 'mean' something, because we, as a community of English-speaking folks decided on this *thusness*.

But how was this decision made? Arbitrarily. The main religions of the world will try to convince you that such decisions are made in heaven. Words are sacred and belong to God. Right. I see Moses descending the mountain with the tablets. It was actually an anthropologist who said that writing was invented for the sole purpose to enslave people. Look around. The dimwitted take the written word at face value, as if it has substance. Some are also very particular with writing their vows to recite in church when they say, 'I do.' Conversely, what does it mean to say that *nothing* has substance? How can we understand this, when 'understanding' is also devoid of substance?

Glorious cards. Let's look at images instead of words: the Fool walks into the house of conventions, only to find out that the Tower doesn't have the last say in it. Death does. So nothing has substance because everything dies. Everything is impermanent.

Nothing is permanent. That includes *you*, or the notion of *you*. If you can remember that, you will remember that just as *you* don't last, nor does all that you cling to last – including *you* as a story. Why you as a story? Because *you* is nothing but a story. *You* has no more substance than the three letters of *you* put together. You can check the veracity of the Buddha's lesson here by reflecting on how you react to my words. If you find it tedious, then search for the point of reference for your existence. If *you* is not the sum of constructs, you should not be able to have any sentiments whatsoever vis-à-vis what I have to say. In other words, there should be no provocation, if *you* is above culture and affect.

The impenetrable obvious is death. Death is the answer to the greatest mysteries. You're happy? It will pass. You are miserable? It will pass. If anybody has agency, it's time. That is to say, the time that only exists as a quantifiable idea in the head, for it doesn't exist otherwise.

If anybody has control, it is change itself that has control. Ergo: Relax. If you think of the impermanence of all things, it's impossible not to arrive at this realization, namely, that there is nothing you can do that you are not doing already, and that it is perfect.

There's a catch for this perfection, however, as it takes just the clear mind to get to the realization that since life is on a default course, all that we do in between the events manifest in the basic idea that we get born, we live, and we die is just a manifestation of being culturally attached to an image of the self and ideology.

## PRAJÑĀPĀRAMITĀ

*The Perfection of Understanding* or *Heart of the Perfection of Wisdom* is a Buddhist apocrypha text written in China, ca. 609 CE. Here is an example of the Sanskrit manuscript of *The Heart Sutra* held at the Bibliothèque nationale de France, 6th C.

The original text is called *The Great Mother,* containing ca. 100,000 lines. Over time, the text got abbreviated, and now it exists in different sizes, ranging considerably from 1 word to 25,000 lines: One Letter Sutra (A); The Heart Sutra (280 words); Diamond Cutting Sutra (concise); the 8,000, 18,000, 20,000, 25,000 line Sutras form a total of 18 Sutras. The 8,000 line sutra is considered the most significant text in the Mahayana tradition.

What does the legend say? The historical Buddha, Shakyamuni Buddha (ca. 563 BC–483 BC) gave radical teachings in installments. These are called 'turnings of the wheel'. The first turning of the wheel delivered at the Deer Park in Sarnath, Northern India, revolves around the 4 noble truths, namely: the truth of suffering; the truth of the cause of suffering; the truth of the end of suffering; and the truth of the path that leads to the end of suffering.

The Buddha, being a wise one, identified the cause of suffering with desire. How to stop suffering? Stop desiring. Just stop it. Stop it and you won't suffer anymore. Isn't this beautiful? I get a kick out of talking about stopping desire at psychoanalytic conferences, which are all about desire. On one such occasion, good friend, professor of literature, and famed psychoanalyst, Robert Silhol, blurted at me: 'what do you mean by ending desire? That means death.' I laughed and said: 'exactly. Imagine being dead while alive.' I think he thought I was a little crazy. Little did he know...

The second and the third turning of the wheel form the teachings of Mahayana school of Buddhism, refined by Tibetan monks. These events happened publicly some 400 years after Shakyamuni's death. The Buddha himself prophesied the belatedness of the delivery of the second and third turnings of the wheel, due to his insight that civilization was not ready for the perfection of wisdom, anchored in the reality of no-substance, the elusiveness of truth, and transmundane experience.

The myth has it that snakes and dragons hid the teachings, until Nagarjuna, 1st c. CE, (*naga*, water spirit in snake form), after having been abducted to the underworld, was given permission to teach the sutras of transcending the self.

Western scholars beg to disagree. There were no dragons or water spirits. Just monks tired of 400 years of harsh self-discipline, needing some love and compassion. I prefer the snake story... It is reported that when the monks heard the third turning of the wheel delivered at the Vulture Peak in Bihar, India, for an audience of bodhisattva they fainted. Some actually had heart attacks, which is slightly worse than fainting.

The language of the turning of the wheels is found in the famous text called, *The Sutra Unraveling the Thought*. There is consensus among scholars and practitioners alike that *The Heart Sutra*, for all its impenetrable obviousness, is not for the faint-hearted. You don't just transcend the self by eradicating desire from the psyche. How is this even or ever possible? The monks facing a wall for 9 years might have an answer to that, as for the rest... pray for us.

Now, what's so hard about *The Heart Sutra*, and why bother with it if it's so hard? Here's what Buddhist scholar and Sufi mystic Lex Hixon thinks it's helpful to conceptualize, if we want to understand what's going on, in his contemplations on the 8,000 lines *Prajnaparamita* from his celebrated book *Mother of the Buddhas*

29

(1993). He gives us a list of terms that refer to
*The Perfection of Wisdom:*

> unfindable, unthinkable, indescribable,
> indecipherable, indefinable, ungrasp-
> able, unformulatable, inconceivable,
> incomparable, unlocatable, unisolatable,
> unapproachable, unchangeable, un-
> reachable, uncalibratable, unframable,
> uncorrelatable, uncharacterizable, insub-
> stantial, nonperspectival, non-self-ex-
> isting, foundationless, baseless, traceless,
> nameless, pathless, goalless, abodeless,
> stainless, measureless, connectionless,
> relationless (12).

Are you still there? Good. Take a deep
breath before the snakes eat you. So, what *can*
we do in the face of how we define the perfec-
tion of wisdom? Enter a paradox. If we want
to understand what's beyond understanding,
then we must start with the work of negation,
something that *The Heart Sutra* itself specializes

30

in, and we will see this shortly. Meanwhile, it takes a certain courage to set yourself the task, in Hixon's words:

> never to thematize, analyze, review, formulate, represent, project, perceive, isolate, define, grasp, crystallize, reify, concretize, objectify, conceptualize, or personalize, *what is,* simply because reality remains great, profound, ineffable, limitless, boundless, boundaryless, frontierless, divisionless, identityless, infinite, transparent, harmoniously functioning, open, free, elusive, deep, pure, empty, sublime, calmly quiet, at peace, and blissfully awakened (13).

Exactly what I thought. There's a second million dollar question we can now pose. How can we read *The Heart Sutra* without fainting?

Let's bring in the cards and see how we can escape this embarrassment of not getting the idea of the non-substantiality of all things.

THE NOTHING THAT IS. Can we understand this? How? Do we *need* to understand this apart from our desire to entertain ourselves? In my own understanding of life in general, what I have observed is the following: suffering arises when we stake a claim, make a claim, or cling to a claim. We want to win arguments. I live for that myself. But what's it to it? We say, 'in a split of a second, such and such person lost their lives in an avalanche.' 'Over night the Harry Potter woman became a millionaire.' Some call this fate, others call it luck. *The Heart Sutra* would call this nothing. But how is this nothing, when we can count our blessings or quantify our time in misery?

The Hanged Man, Justice, and the Tower suggest the following: there is nothing that can prevent you from crashing. Once you give yourself over to Reality – and it's not like you have a choice – you're here now, reading this – there's nothing that can prevent you from experiencing all that you have built around yourself as crashing down. Reality – truth, justice, cosmic karma – by whatever name, cares little about your protective man-made bricks. We're definitely in for some fainting. Sorry about that.

Brace yourself then. You have been warned. Here comes *The Heart Sutra* in an inedit rendition, glowing and radiating. I don't know of anyone else having done this, read the sutra with some cards for fun and to get better at card reading too, so consider yourself lucky...

As you can imagine, there are countless translations of *The Heart Sutra*. But here is my favorite, a Japanese 'transcreation' by poet Hiromi Ito, a woman who writes about children and aging. Her creative translation is of the 'original' Chinese text, translated again into English from Japanese by Jeffrey Angles (Vagabond Press).

The original text is a dialogue between the enlightened bodhisattva Avalokitesvara and the monk Shariputra, seeking wisdom. Avalokitesvara begins with disclosing right from the beginning that the five 'aggregates' of form, feeling, volition, perception, and consciousness are empty and illusory as is everything else without exception. This is the fundamental Buddhist insight.

In what follows I read *The Heart Sutra* by breaking it up into four parts. After each part I pause to take a breath with the cards. I ask a question based on what I find moving in the read passage, and then lay down three cards.

First I devise the question, and then I let the cards fall on the table completely at random. For each passage I shuffle the major arcana anew. This is a completely personal method for me that I have designed in the name of appreciation; appreciation of the way random-ness mediates quite literally between the visual language of the cards and the verbal articulation of the fundamental principle in Buddhism that I find the greatest and most helpful: the idea of no substance, no self-existence. The cards didn't surprise, yet I'm in awe. Here's the first part of *The Heart Sutra* in Hiromi Ito's words:

*While looking freely and without effort at*
*the world*
*While walking with people, searching for the*
*path*
*In his spiritual quest to discern based on deep*
*wisdom*
*Avalokiteshvara arrived at a certain thought.*
*The self is. All sorts of things are.*
*I sense that*
*I recognize that*
*I think about that*
*And it is the case that*
*In all things we discern*
*We are ourselves.*
*However, that means*
*Those things do not exist*
*I have understood that clearly*
*And I have escaped*
*All suffering and trouble.*

Let us now pose this question to the cards, in order to see how we might understand these first lines in *The Heart Sutra* with the help of the visual language of the tarot: *while looking freely and without effort at the world, what do we see that's related to how things do not exist?*

The World, the Fool, and the Hermit say the following: the only thing we see is our method of going about it. The World arises as it does, freely, indeed – thank you cards.

We start questioning: What is 'world?' What is 'freedom?' What is my own speculative mind, weary of the world's ways? What is the nature of all things? If I can ask this question about the nature of all things, does this

very question not prove already that nothing
has substance beyond the words we come up
with to constitute it?

*Listen to this, Shariputra.*
*Being is not any different than non-being.*
*Non-being is not any different than being.*
*Things we think are really are not.*
*If we think of something as non-being that*
*leads to being.*
*Sensing*
*Recognizing*
*Thinking*
*Discerning*
*Those things too are just as they are.*
*Listen to this, Shariputra.*
*All things that are, are not.*
*There is also no living or dying.*
*There is also no dirty or clean.*
*There is also no increasing or decreasing.*

Here's my question to the cards for this part:
*how is being not different than non-being?*

LE·PAPE          LE·FOV          LA·PAPESSE

The Pope, the Fool, and the Popess make an
appearance – note how the Fool, the accidental
Zen person shows up twice in a row here. What
does this string of cards suggest?

If being is a convention, even a dogmatic
one at that for all its potential claim to divinity
or sacredness, then it is bound to cancel itself
out by virtue of all things being equal. The
Pope may preach awareness, even unawares,
only to run into his opposite: the Popess.

Spoken words are not different than written
words. Words are words. Some bite us in the
ass. Alas.

*To put it another way*
*In* non-being
*There is no* being.
*There is also no* sensing, *no* recognizing
*Also no* thinking, *no* discerning.
*There are also no* eyes, *no* ears, *no* noses, *no* tongues
*Also no* bodies, *no* hearts.
*There are also no* colors, *no* shapes, *no* voices, *no* scents, *no* flavors.
*Also no* tangible things, *no* thought-pro-voking things.
*There is also* no world that can be seen with the eyes.
*There is also* no world that can be sensed by the heart.
*There are various things that arise from the workings of the human heart*
*Ranging from the world that can be seen with the eyes*
*To the world that can be sensed by the heart*
*But none of those exist,*
*Yet neither do those workings go away.*

41

*There is also no* suffering of not knowing.
*Nor does the* suffering of not knowing *go away.*
*There is also no* aging, dying, *and* suffering
*Nor does* aging, dying, *and* suffering *go away*
*Because people do not know*
*There are kinds of various kinds of suffering*
*as we grow old and die*
*But none of those exist*
*Yet neither do those sufferings go away.*
*There is also no suffering in living.*
*There is also no confusion that creates suffering.*
*There is also no hope our suffering and our confusion*
*Will one day go away*
*Yet neither is there any effort to rid ourselves*
*Of suffering and confusion.*
*There is no* knowing.
*There is no* gaining.

Assuming that there's still a sense of self that's maintained by the time we finish reading these lines, let's pose this question now to the cards: *where does 'there is no knowing, there is no gaining' leave me?*

The Hermit, the Popess, and the Charioteer answer: you can search for meaning all you want. You can read about meaning all you want. 'What's in it for me?' is not the question. That's not what cuts it. When there is nothing you can know, nothing you can gain, all you've got is moving, your drive. Spin your narratives.

43

Drive into them full force, but do not identify movement with knowing or gaining. Movement is movement.

*In other words, we cannot gain.*
*Therefore.*
*Those who search for the way*
*Follow this wisdom.*
*And then.*
*The things our hearts dwell upon go away.*
*All things we dwell upon go away.*
*Therefore.*
*Fear will go away.*
*All confusion will grow distant,*
*And the heart free of suffering will grow*
*clear.*
*Present, past, future*
*All awakened ones always follow this wisdom*
*They have lived by it and will live by it.*
*And then.*
*It is clearly possible to awaken.*
*Therefore.*
*Know this wisdom that will carry you to the*

*far shore.*
*This is a powerful incantation.*
*This is a powerful incantation that you will*
*hear clearly.*
*This is the ultimate incantation.*
*This is an incantation that knows no equal.*
*All suffering will leave you immediately.*
*This is the truth. This is not a false claim.*
*Therefore.*
*I will tell you this wise incantation.*
*Here, I will tell you. This is how it goes.*
*Gyāte*
*Gyāte*
*Pāra gate*
*Pāra samgate*
*Bodhi svāhā*
*Go, go, go, go beyond, awaken. Thus.*

If this is a powerful incantation, we can
think of it as a spell of enchantment we can cast
on ourselves. Therefore let us now ask this very
question that we can answer with the cards: *how
do I cast a spell of nothingness on myself?*

The Wheel of Fortune, the Sun, and the
Tower fall on the table. It seems that we come
full circle. We started with the Tower and we
ended with the Tower. If there's a reason for
this coincidence, or magic, then we can say that
it might have this function, that we remind
ourselves of this wisdom: 'This too shall pass.'

The Wheel of change turns and turns. You
share yourself with others. But there is no *you*
other than in a conventional, linguistic sense.
You cast a spell of nothingness on yourself by
going beyond the constructed self. *You* exists,
because you experience *you* with all its masks or

nakedness. But this experience has no sub-
stance, no self-existence. We're with the form
we can call spellbinding emptiness.

What can we conclude from this? That
there's no greater spell-work out there than the
spell of nothingness, in the sense that not even
nothingness has substance. Conceptually, noth-
ingness is full of itself, full of the cleverness
imposed on it by the minds that don't know
that they are precisely empty. There's flirtation
with the vertigo that nothingness induces in
us, whenever we try to wrap our heads around
what we gain from knowing. But we heard
it already, there's no knowing and there's no
gaining.

Is your head spinning yet? I hope so. Think
of the demons you may fight with, the demons
who control your fears and desires, the demons
of certitude. If you're empty of everything,
gone beyond, thoroughly beyond, then how do
you suppose the demons can find you to plague
you? If you lost your job or your lover left

you, what of it? How does knowing that this is terrible change the terrible? 'She wrote today, what unimaginable bliss...!' Now you're at the other end of the emotional spectrum. Some call this being alive, being human. Oh, wow, isn't that impressive? Think of what the sages might say. There's no gain. There's no knowing. What if you thought instead that if nothing has substance, then neither the terrible nor the joyful has any substance. Take this to your heart, especially in times of crisis, in times of questioning, and in times of learning too. Cast a spell on your heart.

Next time you read your cards with this in mind, that you're gone beyond, thoroughly beyond, awaken in the suchness of your spell, then ask: how do you suppose that it will *not* be possible to read the cards like the Devil, to think like the Devil, the Devil who possesses all the hearts in *no heart*?

It is *not* possible.

## A Spell on Your Toes

THIS IS YOUR SPELL: The *not* in not knowing. How does it manifest? Wrap yourself up in some warm woollies and while having coffee or a strong drink, meditate on your toes. Then say something similar to the following lines, while maintaining a brave face. You're only on the verge of laughing. You're not laughing yet. How are your toes? You can see them, they exist. You can feel them. They help you with grounding. There's no doubt about the importance of your body.

I think of my body having no substance.
I identify not.
I think of my thoughts having no substance.
I identify not.
I think of my plans having no substance.
I identify not.
I think of love having no substance.
I identify not.
I think of hatred having no substance.
I identify not.
I think of politics having no substance.
I identify not.
I think of transactions having no substance.
I identify not.
I think of insight having no substance.
I identify not.
I think of liberation having no substance.
I identify not.
'It's a good day,' language says.
Tell it to shut up.
*Gate, gate, paragate, parasamgate*
*Bodhi svaha.*

✠

# References

BRUNNHOLZL, Karl (2012). *The Heart Attack Sutra: A new commentary on the Heart Sutra*. Snow Lion.

HIXON, Lex (1993). *Mother of the Buddhas*. Quest Books.

ITO, Hiromi (2016). *Poems of Hiromi Ito, Tashiko Hirata & Takako Arai* (2016). With translations by Jeffrey Angles. Vagabond Press / Asia Pacific Series. Available online at Jacket2.org: "Hiromi Ito's transcreation of 'The Heart Sutra,' by Jerome Rothenberg.